A Taste of Heligan
vegetarian and fruit recipes

RICHARD QUESTED and PAUL DRYE

First published in 2002 by Truran, Croft Prince, Mount Hawke, Truro, Cornwall TR4 8EE
www.truranbooks.co.uk

Reprinted 2002 & 2007

ISBN 978 185022 169 2

Text © Heligan Gardens Ltd
Illustrations © Sue Lewington

Printed and bound in Cornwall by
R. Booth Ltd, Antron Hill, Mabe, Penryn, Cornwall TR10 9HH

Thanks must go to:
the entire catering team at Heligan for their enthusiasm, dedication, energy and all the raucous laughter, but especially to Tina Bishop, Carol Sherwood, Sue Bishop, Katy Warnes, Mary Williams and Duncan Ferguson;
from the gardening team: Katharine of Tarragon, Andrea, Johanna, Charles and Clive;
and all our suppliers whose excellent service and quality we rely upon.

Paul would like to thank Angela for all her patience and typing and Ellie for her devotion.

Richard would like to thank Mel for her love and help with technology and also Luigi Carugati, Brenda and Yvonne for their early inspiration.

The Willows Tearoom/Restaurant is open to non-garden visitors throughout the year from 10am daily, closing half an hour before the gardens. For information about our summer Feast Nights and for bookings, tel 01726 845100.

The gardens are open all year round from 10 am daily.
The Lost Gardens of Heligan, Pentewan, St Austell, Cornwall PL26 6EN
Tel: 01726 845100   www.heligan.com

Introduction

Welcome to our collection of vegetarian recipes.

After meeting at Heligan some years ago we were soon to discover that no matter what fish or meats were on the menu, our beautiful home-grown vegetables were the true stars; and after years of cooking with those very best home-grown ingredients, it now gives us great pleasure to share our favourite recipes with you.

'We' being Richard Quested, who has a passion for organic food and has been living the vegetarian idyll for some years, and Paul Drye, a craft-trained chef with carnivorous leanings, who will cook and eat all manner of fish and meat quite happily. One of us could no more become a vegetarian than the other could eat meat, but despite this contrast we get on very well and a fine culinary balance is achieved. As chefs it is our job to do justice to the fruit, vegetables and the herbs grown here. You will find in this book the best and most popular vegetarian dishes in our repertoire. Most are original with a few Heligan favourites such as Homity Pie, Mushroom and Wild Garlic Soup and Honey-roast Vegetables. Our recipes are placed in seasonal order to take into account the availability of certain ingredients throughout the year.

We feature many of these recipes at our regular Feast Nights during the summer months. We started these with the aim of producing the very best food we possibly could, using the finest ingredients from the garden paired with other high quality produce from local suppliers. This has proved a great opportunity to showcase the epicurean delights of Cornwall; so why not come and experience one of these special occasions for yourself - we would love to see you here.

The enormous daily task we have set ourselves in the kitchen at Heligan would be impossible without the support of the gardening team, whose freshly harvested produce plays such an important part in the construction of our menus. The link between garden and kitchen is crucial, whether we are preparing food for a hundred pre-booked evening guests who dine at leisure, or for the multitude of more casual visitors on an average day. What we cook revolves around what is available from the productive gardens, where a huge range of mostly traditional varieties of fruits, vegetables and herbs are planted in an on-going cycle and nurtured by our dedicated staff. Crop after crop is then lifted or cut; the harvest is brought home and wheelbarrows full of the freshest ingredients come to our kitchen door. What more could we ask?

Fresh ingredients are always best. We have only to compare the experience of eating a 'so-called' fresh melon or peach from our local supermarket (harvested when unripe, in another country and transported perhaps thousands of miles) with the pure joy of indulging in a succulent fruit from one of our glasshouses here at Heligan - picked and eaten within minutes and bursting with flavour and juices: this is an experience altogether on another level. Every vegetable gardener can testify to this truth.

In compiling what follows we did not aim to teach people how to cook. There are so many other good cookery books, which describe the basic skills of food preparation. The purpose of this little book is to celebrate the joys of eating fresh, locally-produced food. Buying local means buying ingredients that are local to you. If you search around you will be amazed at what you can find - and while exploring what is available in your own locality you may also discover a rich culinary heritage with exciting regional specialities. We are very proud of the many Cornish ingredients that we use in our recipes; but remember that the key to buying the freshest produce is to search your own area.

The recipes here are really just to be used as a guide, as rules are made to be broken. So if you are unable to get hold of a particular ingredient, it is not the end of the world; just adapt the recipe to suit by replacing it with something similar. Any cook would agree that the secret to a successful dish is to start with the freshest ingredients - you cannot beat home-grown produce. Having said this, these recipes are not set in stone. We all know fresh herbs are best but at a pinch, dried herbs will do. Fresh tomatoes bring great flavour to many dishes but, in your busy life, using a tin of chopped tomatoes is no great sin. What is important is that you have a great time cooking and an even better time eating. Good food is very important, but when mixed with good wine, good music and good company, life can't get much better.

RICHARD QUESTED & PAUL DRYE
Catering Manager & Head Chef
The Lost Gardens of Heligan

The Recipes

Soups and Starters

Main Courses

Accompaniments and Salads

Puddings

Oils, Dressings and Preserves

Mushroom and Wild Garlic Soup

One of the best things about spring for me at Heligan is to be able to take sojourns down to the Jungle, returning sometime later with armfuls of wild garlic (ramsons) and very muddy feet. These deliciously pungent leaves are paired beautifully with our home-grown mushrooms in this - one of my favourite - soups. At Heligan we grow our own mushrooms in a dark house, cropping throughout the year.

For 6-8

900g/2lb sliced mushrooms
170g/6oz onion
110g/4oz celery
 - all chopped quite finely
about 1140mls/2 pints vegetable stock
1 large sprig of fresh parsley
1 large bunch of ramson leaves, washed
225mls/8fl oz double cream
1 tablespoon olive oil
2 tablespoons cornflour mixed with a little water
salt and pepper

Take a large saucepan (2.25 litres/4 pints) and heat the olive oil. To this, add the finely chopped onion and celery and cook gently until the onion is soft. Then in go the mushrooms (this looks quite a lot of mushrooms, but this is fine) - cover with vegetable stock and season with a little salt and pepper. You can always add more at the end. Simmer this for an hour giving it an occasional stir. This gives you time to finely shred the ramson leaves and chop the parsley. While the soup is still simmering, gradually add the cornflour mix, stirring all the time. Pour in the cream and add the parsley and ramsons, slowly bring back to a simmer, have a taste, correct the seasoning and serve.

We make our own bread to go with this, but if you don't have the time, any of the Italian style breads from your local supermarket will suit very well.

Leek and Herb Consommé

This soup makes good use of whatever fresh herbs you have growing and can be very different according to which herbs you use. The leeks give it a beautiful hint of sweetness, counteracted by the savoury flavour of the herbs. It is a light and refreshing soup which is ideal as a starter in a 3 course meal, or as part of a 5 course meal if you are feeling extravagant.

For 4-6

For stock:
1 tablespoon olive oil
4 potatoes
2 carrots
1 large onion
1 stick celery
1 bay leaf
1420mls/2½ pints water

For soup:
1-2 leeks
selection of herbs
few drops of balsamic vinegar
1 tablespoon olive oil
salt and pepper

Roughly chop all the vegetables for the stock to begin your soup. Heat the oil and sweat the vegetables for 5-10 minutes. Do not let them brown. Add the water, bring to the boil, cover and simmer for around 2 hours. Allow to cool and strain. This is the basic consommé for the soup.

Next shred the leeks finely and fry gently for 5 minutes. Add the stock and bring it to the boil. Chop the herbs: parsley, coriander, mint, chervil, and basil are all good, but use whatever you fancy. Place the chopped herbs into warm serving dishes and pour the hot consommé onto them. Leave for a few minutes to infuse, add 2-3 drops balsamic vinegar (optional) and serve.

Asparagus with Sweet Marjoram Butter

There are a number of reasons at Heligan to use local suppliers: promoting and supporting local businesses as well as giving visitors a taste of Cornwall. For me though, the best thing about buying locally is the freshness of the produce. This food has not travelled long distances over land and sea. Often, the time between harvesting and eating can be hours rather than days or even weeks. Asparagus spears should be used as fresh as possible, preferably within an hour of picking. Luckily we grow the best asparagus here at Heligan - only a ten minute walk from the kitchen - this truly is Chef's Heaven.

For 4

24-48 asparagus spears
1 small bunch of marjoram
55g/2oz butter
salt

Firstly make the marjoram butter. Start by softening the butter for a few seconds in a microwave or by leaving at room temperature; then mix in the washed and finely chopped marjoram and return to the fridge. The asparagus should have the tough ends removed and, if required, the bottom third of the stems peeled with a fine potato peeler to remove any woodiness from the outer skin. Tie the asparagus into bundles and simmer gently in lightly salted water, standing upright with the tips out of the water. Cover with a lid and cook for 8-12 minutes until 'al dente' (the tips will be cooked in the steam). Remove from the water; drain and serve immediately with a knob of sweet marjoram butter melting over the top. Alternatively, for a luxurious Sunday breakfast, dip them like soldiers into a couple of soft-boiled eggs.

Carrot, Orange and Coriander Soup

What a summery soup this is! You can even serve this chilled with ice and a slice of orange. In the summer months, fragrant bunches of coriander arrive from the productive gardens. This wonderful herb finishes the soup perfectly, while the smell of freshly chopped coriander always gives me irresistible cravings for Indian food!

For 6-8

450g/1lb carrots
450g/1lb tomatoes
170g/6oz onion
4 large oranges
1140mls/2 pints vegetable stock
generous bunch of fresh coriander leaves
2 teaspoons sugar
1 tablespoon sunflower oil
salt and pepper

Firstly heat the oil in a large pan, then add the onion, carrot and tomatoes, all peeled and roughly chopped. (To peel tomatoes, cut a cross in the bottom and immerse in boiling water for 1 minute; then immerse in cold water and they should peel easily). Cook gently for 10 minutes, then add the vegetable stock and the juice and zest of 4 oranges. Bring to the boil; add the sugar, then season with a little salt and pepper. Simmer until all the vegetables are tender; while all this simmering is going on, you can roughly chop the coriander and resist phoning your local Indian take-away! Purée the soup in a liquidizer, adjust the seasoning if required, and return to the heat. Stir in the coriander at the last minute (if cooked for too long this herb loses some of its vitality and the flavour is impaired) - serve immediately.

Any freshly-baked bread or even cinnamon toast goes very well with this.

Cinnamon Toast - Cut some bread into 4 triangles. Mix some butter with cinnamon and a little icing sugar; butter the bread and bake in the oven until crisp and golden.

Twice Baked Village Green Soufflés with Beetroot Crisps

Using this traditional Cornish hard goat's cheese and a sinful amount of our own fresh chives gives a local twist to these wonderfully rich little soufflés. Cooked a few hours before serving they are then re-baked at the last minute, accompanied by beetroot crisps with cracked sea salt. These are a big hit in the summer and, as most of the hard work is done in advance, you will arrive at the table cool and calm, while the soufflés are hot and steamy!

For 6

140g/5oz grated Village Green cheese
290mls/10fl oz milk
55g/2oz plain flour
55g/2oz butter
pinch nutmeg
pinch Cayenne pepper
pinch salt
pinch black pepper
large pinch English mustard powder
55g/2oz chopped fresh chives
3 large eggs - separated
190mls/7fl oz single cream
225g/8oz uncooked beetroot
cracked sea salt

Heat the milk slowly in a pan with a pinch of nutmeg. Melt the butter in a second pan and stir in the flour to make a roux. Gradually add the milk, stirring briskly until smooth and thickened. Remove from the heat and stir in the Cayenne, salt, pepper, mustard, chives, 85g/3oz of the Village Green cheese and finally stir in the egg yolks.

Whisk the egg whites until they reach medium peak stage and with a metal spoon carefully fold in to the mixture, retaining as much air as possible. Share the mixture between 6 well-buttered ramekins or ovenproof cups. Place them in a roasting pan and half fill with boiling water, then bake in a preheated oven 180°C/350°F/gas 4 for 15-20 minutes until set. Remove from the oven and allow to cool. Turn out the soufflés and place upside down in an ovenproof dish. Twenty minutes before serving, pour over the cream, evenly coating each soufflé. Sprinkle the remaining cheese over the top and bake in a hot oven 220°C/425°F/gas 7 for 10-12 minutes until puffed up and light golden in colour. Serve immediately before they sink.

To make the crisps simply peel and thinly slice the beetroot, pat dry on kitchen paper and deep fry in hot oil until crisp. Turn onto kitchen paper for a few minutes, give a generous sprinkle of cracked sea salt and serve. These can also be made in advance.

Ambervale and Wild Mushroom Parcels

I had made filo parcels before using spinach and Ricotta, served both as a starter and as a main course. This is the same idea, but with a Cornish twist, using a locally produced cheese and wild mushrooms. Late summer through to early autumn is a wonderful time to be a chef at Heligan; the numbers of visitors are gently slowing down and wild mushrooms are popping up everywhere. Shaggy ink caps and common puff balls work very well when paired with Ambervale cheese. If you are confident, pick your own mushrooms, but now exotic varieties of mushroom are available in supermarkets.

For 4

450g/1lb wild mushrooms
85g/3oz onion
170g/6oz Ambervale cheese
24 squares filo pastry
quarter teaspoon nutmeg
1 tablespoon olive oil
55g/2oz melted butter
salt and pepper
a little water

A cautionary note - shaggy ink caps are quite distinctive with their shaggy appearance, but common ink caps, although similar in shape, are smooth. These, although edible, when mixed with alcohol produce some very unpleasant side effects, so I only eat the shaggy ink caps and the wine flows freely.

Heat the oil in a saucepan, adding the finely sliced onion along with the wiped and sliced mushrooms. Cook slowly for 5-10 minutes, then drain off any liquid. Grate the Ambervale and place in a bowl, then mix in the cooked and cooled mushrooms with a little salt and pepper to taste. Place one square of filo pastry on a lightly floured table, brush with water and place another sheet on top but offset from the first sheet, brush with a little water and place a third sheet, again offset from the last. Spoon a mound of the filling onto the middle of the pastry, brush water around the outside edge of the filo, then gather all the corners and bunch together at the top, giving a firm pinch to secure the parcel. Transfer to a greased baking sheet and brush with melted butter. Repeat this until you have 8 parcels, allowing 2 per person. Bake in a moderately hot oven, preheated to 200°C/400°F/gas 6 for 10-14 minutes or until golden brown. Please note if there is too much liquid left in the mushrooms, the parcels may burst open. These go well with many things: a salad, stir-fried vegetables or even a basil and green olive risotto would suit very nicely.

Baba Ghanoush

Baba Ghanoush - what a wonderful name - is an aubergine purée, served as part of the 'mezze' tradition in Turkey and Greece. Mezze comes from the Persian word 'maza', meaning taste or relish. The possible origins of mezze go back to ancient Persia, where wine was the centre of an emotional and aesthetic experience also including other forms of enjoyment, notably food and music. Sounds jolly good to me. Baba Ghanoush is also known as the 'poor man's caviar' and traditionally is served with pitta bread or crudités. A delicious appetizer.

For 4-6

2-3 large aubergines
2-3 cloves garlic
1 small onion
juice of 2 lemons
120mls/4fl oz tahini
large bunch parsley
1 tablespoon olive oil

Preheat the oven to 230°C/450°F/gas 8. Bake the aubergines for around 30 minutes until the skins are black and blistered. Allow to cool slightly, then peel off the charred skin and roughly chop the aubergine flesh. Peel and crush the garlic, finely chop the onion and put in a blender with the aubergine and a large pinch of salt. Blend lightly and then add the tahini, alternating with the lemon juice, giving a whizz of the blender at each stage. Finish off by adding the chopped parsley. Stir and then chill for at least 2 hours, to allow the flavours to develop. Drizzle with olive oil to serve.

Chick-a-Leekie Soup

The leeks we grow here have a very long season and the gardeners arrive with wheelbarrows full on a regular basis. When cooked well, leeks take on a really sweet flavour and are great in just about everything, from light quiches to hearty casseroles. The idea for this soup came to me one day when Richard (Veggie) said about my Cock-a-Leekie soup "that smells good - shame about the chicken!" - so here's the vegetarian alternative:

For 6-8

675g/1lb 8oz leeks
110g/4 oz onion
110g/4oz dried prunes (pitted)
110g/4oz chickpeas (soaked for 24 hours)
1140mls/2 pints vegetable stock
110g/4oz butter
110g/4oz flour
sprig each of parsley, marjoram, thyme
salt and pepper

Sometime before, drain the soaked chickpeas and boil in fresh water until tender (this can take a couple of hours). Meanwhile, heat the butter in a large saucepan (2.25 litres/4 pints), and slowly cook off the onions and leek, which must be finely sliced, until soft. Mix in the flour and cook out a little. Gradually pour in the vegetable stock, stirring all the time and bring to a steady simmer. Add the finally chopped herbs and the drained, cooked chickpeas and continue simmering for half an hour - not forgetting to give it a stir now and again. Chop the dried prunes and add them to the soup. These are the traditional but often forgotten ingredient in cock-a-leekie soup. Cook for a further 10 minutes, season to taste and serve. If you wish, a little cream could be stirred in at the end.

This delicious soup is even better served with hunks of nutty, wholemeal bread.

Pumpkin, Roast Pepper & Coriander Paté

Another Feast Night favourite, and very simple to make. We are lucky enough to have all the main ingredients for this wonderful vegetarian paté home-grown at Heligan. It really is a joy to serve a dish that is 100% Heligan produced!

For 4-6

225g/8oz pumpkin flesh
1 red pepper
1 yellow pepper
1 green pepper
225g/8oz red onion
4 cloves garlic
110g/4oz wholemeal bread
3 tablespoons olive oil
1 teaspoon soy sauce
6 sprigs rosemary
6 sprigs parsley
1 large bunch coriander leaves
salt and pepper

Roughly chop the pumpkin, peppers, red onion and garlic. Put them in a roasting tin. Then mix in a jug the olive oil, soy sauce, a little salt and pepper and the rosemary removed from its stalk. Drizzle the oil mixture over the vegetables and roast in a preheated oven at 200°C/400°F/gas 6 for half an hour, when the pumpkin should be tender. (I say should, because some varieties of pumpkin can be firmer than others). When cooked, remove from the oven and leave to cool for a while until safe to handle. Then whizz the vegetables in a food processor along with pieces of wholemeal bread. Don't whizz too much though, as the paté looks much better having a coarser texture. Then stir in all the coriander finely chopped. Taste and adjust the seasoning if required, and spoon into ramekins, garnishing with sprigs of fresh parsley.

We served these generously heaped onto homemade oat cakes. A very moreish vegetarian starter with an explosion of flavours!

Cream of Pumpkin and Spinach Soup

At Heligan we grow many varieties of pumpkins and squashes. When I first took my family to Heligan, my two sons, Jay and Max, were absolutely gob-smacked by the squashes - the huge selection of shapes, sizes and colours. There are orange, red, yellow, blue, green, beige and white; fat, thin, round, oval, smooth, warty, bumpy, ridged and huge through to tiny - all sorts.
This soup has a velvety texture, delicate flavour, and the spinach adds lovely flecks of colour.

For 4-6

55g/2oz butter
2 cloves garlic
3 medium onions
30g/1oz root ginger
900g/2lb pumpkin flesh
850mls/1½ pints vegetable stock
290mls/½ pint single cream
110g/4oz spinach

Melt the butter in a pan and then add the crushed garlic and ginger, chopped onions and diced pumpkin flesh. Cover and leave to sweat on a low heat for around 15 minutes. Check often and give a stir so that nothing browns or sticks. Next add the vegetable stock, bring up to the boil and then simmer gently for 15-20 minutes until the pumpkin is tender. Leave to cool a little and then purée the mixture in a food processor and return to the pan. Season with the nutmeg, salt and pepper. Shred the spinach very finely, add to the soup and gently bring it back to just below boiling point, by which time the spinach will be cooked. Stir in the cream and serve immediately.

Curried Parsnip and Apple Soup

When people think of curried soups mulligatawny comes to mind, but often this soup is too fiery. This is a subtle alternative with delicate but pronounced flavours, plus, parsnip and apple are such a great team together. Recently I made a parsnip and apple cake (that's right, parsnip!) using an old carrot cake recipe - and very good it was too.

For 6-8

560g/1lb 4oz parsnips
170g/6oz onion
4 cloves garlic
1 large cooking apple
55g/2oz creamed coconut
1140mls/2 pints vegetable stock
1 tablespoon sunflower oil
8 teaspoons mild curry powder
1 teaspoon black mustard seeds
1 teaspoon ground coriander
1 teaspoon ground fenugreek
110mls/4 fl oz double cream or yoghurt
sprig fresh coriander leaves
30g/1oz toasted flaked almonds
salt and pepper

Heat the oil in a large pan (2.25 litres/4 pints), add the spices, diced onion and crushed garlic and fry for 5 minutes. Then add the coconut and vegetable stock and bring to the boil. Peel and roughly chop the parsnip and apple and add to the soup, followed by a good pinch of salt. Simmer until the parsnips are tender, then remove from heat. Whizz in a blender until smooth, return to the heat stirring in the cream or yoghurt. Taste and season if required. Serve with toasted almonds and roughly chopped coriander sprinkled on top.

What type of bread to have with this? It has to be naan of course!

Allium Compote Ravioli

Although this recipe looks quite complicated, in practice it is deliciously simple and well worth the effort. We have used this allium compote in many recipes and it makes an intense filling for these little tomato pasta parcels. Then, when tossed in a rich red pesto, it makes a great starter or main course. You can also use the pasta recipe for many other dishes.

For 4

Filling:
1 leek
1 red onion
2 cloves garlic
2 spring onions
1 small bunch chives
1 tablespoon olive oil
30g/1oz fresh bread crumbs
salt and pepper

Pasta:
450g/1lb strong '00' flour
4 eggs
1 tablespoon olive oil
2 teaspoons tomato purée

Wash and finely chop the leek, red onion, garlic, spring onions and chives. Heat the oil, add these ingredients to the pan and slowly cook without colour. Cover with a close fitting lid. Continue cooking until completely soft. Remove lid and reduce until quite thick, stirring frequently, finally adding the breadcrumbs; season with salt and pepper and then leave to cool.

Sift the flour onto a clean table, make a well in the centre, then crack the eggs into the well, adding the oil and tomato purée. Using one hand, mix together gradually, drawing in the flour until a stiff dough is reached. Knead until smooth and elastic. Wrap in cling film and chill for 1 hour. Roll out the pasta dough quite thinly and cut circles with a small round biscuit cutter. Spoon a small mound of filling in the centre, brush water around the edge, place a second round of pasta on the top and seal around the edges. Continue thus until all the pasta is used up. Leave to dry for at least 30 minutes on a wire rack. Then gently simmer the pasta in lightly salted water for 12-15 minutes. Drain and serve tossed in red pesto (see recipe page 47), on a bed of Flora's Green Salad. (see recipe page 31)

Chard and Yarg Quiche

This is a super way of using the many varieties of Chard that are grown here in great abundance. These include rainbow, Swiss and ruby chard. All are wonderful as a vegetable to accompany a main dish, but here they are stepping into the limelight paired with Yarg, my favourite Cornish cheese (a wonderful nettle-wrapped hard cheese indigenous to Cornwall). Not only does the name 'Chard and Yarg' have a nice ring to it, but also, when you slice into this quiche a beautiful marble effect appears, created by the chard leaves.

For 4-6

225g/8oz plain flour
110g/4oz butter
splash of cold water
pinch of salt
420mls/15fl oz full cream milk
4 eggs
½ teaspoon English mustard
4 drops of soy sauce
2 teaspoons of freshly chopped parsley
salt and pepper
340g/12oz chard leaves
110g/4oz grated Yarg
1 tablespoon olive oil

Start with the pastry. Rub together the flour, butter and a pinch of salt until a sandy texture is reached, then add just enough water to bring the mixture to a smooth paste (not too sticky, not too dry). Rest for 10 minutes in a fridge, then roll out and use to line a 20cm/8 inch greased quiche dish and refrigerate for a further 10 minutes to relax the pastry. During this time crack the eggs into a mixing bowl, add the milk, mustard, soy sauce, parsley and a little salt and pepper. Whisk until evenly mixed together. Wash, drain and roughly shred the chard leaves (the stalks can be used in soups and casseroles). Take your pastry base and evenly spread out the chard with grated Yarg on top. Then top with the quiche mixture. Bake in quite a low oven preheated to 150°C/300°F/gas 2 for 1-1¼ hours until the egg mixture has set. This can be served hot or cold as a main course, or use a small slice on its own as a starter.

Steak Mushrooms with West Country Brie

Mushrooms and Brie are a wonderful combination - the rich, dark flavour of the mushrooms complimented perfectly by the creamy, sharpness of the brie. We use a West Country Brie which has a good full flavour, but never be afraid to experiment. A very simple and flavoursome dish.

For 4

4 large steak mushrooms
225g/8oz Brie
55g/2oz sunflower seeds
30g/1oz butter
salt and freshly milled pepper

Remove the stalks from the mushrooms, chop finely and mix with the butter. Divide between the mushroom heads and place in the centre of each. Sprinkle the sunflower seeds over the mushrooms, season well and then slice up the Brie and use to cover each mushroom. Cook in a lightly greased baking dish for approximately 15 minutes at 180C/350F/gas 4.

Homity Pie

This is one of our real favourites and a best seller in the Heligan Restaurant. It first appeared in The Heligan Vegetable Bible. *Paul's addition to this recipe is a touch of luxury - cream. A recipe with endless variations (as most are) and we have served it containing mushrooms, roasted vegetables and even (although it has no place in this book) bacon. I will leave all that up to you though!*

For 4-6

170g/6oz shortcrust pastry
675g/1½ lb unpeeled waxy potatoes
2 medium onions
olive oil
4 cloves garlic
170g/6oz mature Cheddar cheese
4 tablespoons chopped flat leaf parsley
sea salt and freshly ground black pepper
150mls/5fl oz double cream

Line a 20cm/9 inch flan tin with the pastry and bake blind for 5 minutes. Cover the potatoes with cold water, bring to the boil and simmer for 10-15 minutes until just cooked, then drain and set aside. Meanwhile roughly chop the onions, crush the garlic and sweat off gently in some olive oil until translucent. Next, slice the potatoes into a large bowl in 5mm/¼ inch slices and mix in the onions, parsley, cream and half of the cheese. Season well. Put loosely into the pastry case, top with the remaining cheese and cook for 20-25 minutes at 190°C/375°F/gas 5. Very tasty either hot or cold.

Mushroom Korma

Many people think of curries as hot, fiery dishes that have no real flavour, but just a burning sensation. A korma is a mild creamy curry that can change a non-curry eater's mind. Paul and myself are both great advocates of Indian food and have had some real fun cooking up curries for Indian nights at Heligan. On one occasion I insisted on listening to Ravi Shankar with Yehudi Menuhin to get that authentic cultural cross-over feel in the kitchen, although I don't think all the staff appreciated this. This dish goes particularly well with Paul's Lemon and Coriander Pilaff.

For 4-6

3-4 cloves garlic
3 medium onions
3-4 teaspoons mild curry powder
1 teaspoon ground coriander
1 teaspoon ground cumin
2 teaspoons turmeric
110g/4oz creamed coconut
110g/4oz ground almonds
2 tablespoons mango chutney
850mls/1½ pints vegetable stock
675g/1½ lb button mushrooms
1 tablespoon sunflower oil or ghee
120mls/4fl oz double cream or yogurt
1 small sprig chopped coriander leaves

Peel and crush the garlic, chop the onions and sweat off in sunflower oil or ghee (clarified butter) for 5-10 minutes until translucent. Add all the spices and fry for about 2 minutes to bring out the flavours of the spices. Now add the vegetable stock, mango chutney, creamed coconut and ground almonds and leave to cook slowly for around 45 minutes. While the sauce is cooking you need to cook the mushrooms. Button mushrooms tend to be best as they do not seem to produce as much liquid. Fry the mushrooms in a little sunflower oil or ghee and then add to the sauce. Stir in the natural yoghurt or cream and garnish with chopped coriander before serving.

Creamy Leek Mille-feuille

This is a deliciously creamy dish with delicate puff pastry and of course, some very fine leeks, full of flavour and cooked slowly to develop a subtle sweetness. We are very lucky here, with impressive regimented rows of leeks in the Vegetable Garden available much of the year.

For 4

675g/1lb 8oz leeks
290mls/10fl oz vegetable stock
450g/1lb puff pastry (shop bought is very good)
1 egg
55g/2oz plain flour
55g/2oz butter
290mls/10fl oz milk
150mls/5fl oz double cream
1/2 teaspoon wholegrain Dijon mustard
pinch of Cayenne pepper
8 chive stems
salt and pepper

Firstly roll out the puff pastry and cut 8 circles with a large round biscuit cutter. Place them on a lightly greased baking tray, brush with beaten egg and bake in a preheated oven at 200°C/400°F/gas 6 for about 15 minutes, until crisp and golden. Remove from the oven and leave to cool on a wire rack.

Wash the leeks and cut into 50mm/2inch lengths. Place in a roasting dish along with the vegetable stock and braise for 20-30 minutes in a preheated oven 200°C/400°F/gas 6. While this is cooking, melt the butter in a saucepan, add the flour and cook out for 3 minutes, stirring continuously. This gives you a roux. Gradually pour in the milk, stirring all the while to stop lumps forming. Add the cream in the same manner. When simmering and thickened, add the mustard, Cayenne pepper and season. (If you are unfortunate enough to have lumps, don't worry, just pass the sauce through a sieve). Drain the leeks thoroughly in a colander, saving the liquid to use as a stock elsewhere, and assemble the mille-feuilles onto four hot plates. Working briskly, slice in half (horizontally) each round of puff pastry and layer in this order: pastry/leeks/sauce 3 times, and finally the last pastry top - this should therefore give you four layers. Repeat this on each plate and garnish with two chive stems crossed and leaning against the mille-feuilles. Serve with new potatoes and roast vegetables, or a Chilli and Lime Pilaff, speckled with diced red pepper.

Honey-roast Vegetables

This dish can be served on its own as a main course with couscous, bulgur wheat, or maybe a risotto. It is also an excellent choice to accompany meat or fish. The recipe changes with the seasons. You can use endless combinations of vegetables and you can also experiment by infusing the oil with herbs and spices, but this recipe will give you a good starting point. Honey-roast Vegetables are often served at the Willows Restaurant here at Heligan. It is a quick and simple dish to prepare and so popular that when it isn't on the menu, there is much disappointment!

For 4

1 large aubergine
1 red pepper
1 green pepper
1 yellow pepper
2 courgettes
1 red onion
110g/4oz button mushrooms
120mls/4fl oz olive oil
2 tablespoons clear honey
2 teaspoons Dijon mustard
6 sprigs rosemary
1 teaspoon celery seeds
a good pinch of salt

Place the olive oil, honey, mustard, celery seeds and rosemary (having removed the tough stalk) in a jug and mix together. Roughly chop the vegetables into quite large chunks and spread out in a roasting tin. Pour the honey mixture over them and roll the vegetables around until they are evenly coated. Sprinkle with a good pinch of salt and roast in a moderately hot oven preheated to 200°C/400°F/gas 6 for 20-30 minutes until the vegetables are browned and caramelised at the edges but still quite firm to bite. Serve piping hot.

Main Courses

Mediterranean Stuffed Aubergine

Aubergines have recently been grown experimentally here at Heligan, and so it is a real treat when they come our way. I feel that because they are something of a rare commodity it seems a shame to include them in a dish like ratatouille, where they would just be lost. This recipe makes the most of the rare Heligan aubergine and keeps its identity.

For 4

2 large aubergines
110g/4 oz onion
110g/4oz couscous
boiling water (enough to cover the couscous)
4 oranges
10 pitted dates
55g/2oz mixed chopped nuts
1 tablespoon olive oil
large sprigs of basil, oregano, parsley and thyme
4 teaspoons demerara sugar
salt and pepper

Put the couscous in a bowl and cover with boiling water, stir and leave to absorb the water and cool. Remove the stalk, and cut the aubergines in half lengthwise. Scoop out the centre, leaving about half an inch of flesh all round. Finely dice the flesh you have removed and, with the diced onion, fry in olive oil until soft. Add the cooked aubergines and onion to the couscous along with chopped dates. Skin and segment two of the oranges and add to the couscous together with the chopped nuts and roughly chopped herbs (keeping a little back for garnish). Stir the couscous until the ingredients are evenly distributed, taste and adjust the seasoning. Spoon into the aubergine halves. Place the stuffed aubergines on a greased baking tray. Peel and slice the last 2 oranges, arranging the slices along the top of the aubergines, sprinkle with demerara sugar and bake for 20-25 minutes in a preheated oven at 200°C/400°F/gas 6.

Serve hot, accompanied by a Greek-style salad with Feta cheese and black olives and a slice of Italian-style ramson bread.

Heligan Bean Bourguignonne

The obvious attraction of being a chef at Heligan is the copious amount of fresh home-grown produce to hand, but at certain times of the year the variety of produce arriving at the kitchen dwindles considerably. From early summer until late autumn we are spoilt for choice but in the leaner months of January and February, with only a few varieties to work with, any previous efforts made by way of preserving, pickling and drying begin to pay dividends. The unusual varieties of pulses and beans look good on the menu and, in this recipe, make a hearty warming dish, perfect for winter evenings.

For 4-6

110g/4oz caseknife beans
110g/4oz two-coloured coco beans
110g/4oz soldier beans (all beans to be soaked separately in cold water overnight)
140g/5oz peeled shallots or button onions
4 cloves crushed garlic
4 plum tomatoes
30g/1oz tomato purée
425mls/15fl oz vegetable stock
150mls/5fl oz red wine
1 bouquet garni (parsley stalks, sprigs of thyme, sprigs of rosemary and a bay leaf sandwiched between a stick of celery and half a leek tied with string)
2 tablespoons plain flour
30g/1oz butter
110g/4oz button mushrooms
small bunch flat-leaf parsley
salt and pepper

Some fresh Heligan produce taxes our culinary expertise to breaking point, the most infamous being the rather unappetising broad bean. The oldest remains of the domesticated broad bean date back to 6800BC and after nearly nine millennia mankind has yet to discover a way of making them palatable. That said, if you have a good recipe for broad beans we would be delighted to hear from you.

Firstly, drain and rinse each type of bean, then boil in 3 separate pans of unsalted water until just tender. When cooking with different varieties of beans it is a good idea to soak and boil them separately as cooking times may vary. Remove from heat and drain through a colander. Heat the butter in a large saucepan, adding the shallots and crushed garlic. Cook for 3 minutes before adding the flour, stir, and continue cooking for another 3 minutes. Slowly pour in the stock, stirring continually to avoid lumps, then add the red wine, tomato puree, tomatoes (roughly chopped) and all of the beans. Stir, season with a little salt and pepper, add the bouquet garni, bring to the boil and cover with a tight fitting lid before placing in a moderate oven 180°C/350°F/gas 4 for 1 hour. Remove from oven, add the mushrooms, remove bouquet garni, check seasoning and add a little water if required. Return to the oven and cook for a further 15 minutes, then serve garnished with snipped flat-leaf parsley. Bean Bourguignonne is excellent with really floury boiled potatoes and baby carrots roasted in a little olive oil and rosemary.

Purple Sprouting Salad

This is a salad for early in the year, before all the vegetables and salad plants have really got going in the garden. Use young, tender purple sprouting broccoli, freshly picked for this salad. Chicory is forced in the dark in the potting shed and is often ready for harvest at the same time.

For 4

225g/8oz purple sprouting broccoli
1-2 heads chicory
2-4 shallots
55g/2oz sun-blushed tomatoes
225g/8oz cooked black-eyed beans
3 tablespoons extra virgin olive oil
1 tablespoon balsamic vinegar
thyme leaves
Dijon mustard

Cut the purple sprouting into small florets, shred the chicory, chop the shallots very finely and mix together with the beans and sun-blushed tomatoes. Mix up the oil and vinegar with the thyme leaves and a little Dijon mustard to make your salad dressing. Use the purple sprouting raw, as when you cook it, it loses its wonderful colour. As long as it is young, it has a crisp texture and a deep flavour.

Dauphinoise Potatoes with Shredded Ramsons

Many of the varieties of potato grown here were previously unknown to me as a chef. Old Victorian varieties have been somewhat forgotten in the 20th century, surpassed by certain well-known commercial varieties. Our supermarkets are full of high yield well-behaved, uniformly shaped potatoes. Luckily the gardeners at Heligan are in a position to play an important role in the conservation of older varieties. As a result I find myself cooking many different potatoes - all with their own taste, colour, texture and character - with names like Ryecroft Purple, Edzell Blue, Shetland Black, Duke of York and May Queen. As for the assignation between Lord Roseberry and the Beauty of Hebron, this is purely a matter of conjecture....

For 4-6

900g/2lb floury old potatoes eg. King Edward
140g/5oz ramson leaves (wild garlic)
30g/1oz parsley
290mls/10fl oz double cream
290mls/10fl oz milk
pinch of salt
freshly ground black pepper

Firstly, wash, peel and re-wash the potatoes, slice them into rounds approximately 6mm/¼ inch thick. Wash and finely shred the ramson leaves, then carefully layer the potato and ramsons in an earthenware dish, finishing with a layer of potatoes. Mix together the cream, milk, parsley and a pinch of salt. Pour this over the potatoes and give a generous twist of black pepper. Cover with foil and bake for one and a half hours in a preheated oven 170°C/325°F/gas 3, removing the foil for the last 20 minutes to brown.

I find this potato dish goes very well with a main course that does not have a sauce, for example, grilled salmon with steamed vegetables. The creaminess of the dauphinoise potatoes just lifts the whole meal.

Champp

An Irish recipe which is a wonderful alternative to plain old mashed potato. On first cooking Victorian varieties of potatoes it was a bit of an adventure; some are quite waxy, some are very floury, then there are the ones that are just coloured blue. Champ is a good way of using potatoes that are a little unstable when boiled. Another option is to make fondant potatoes.

For 4-6

900g/2lb old potatoes
8 spring onions
55g/2oz butter
120mls/4fl oz single cream
pinch of salt
pinch of ground nutmeg
pinch of black pepper

Firstly wash, peel and re-wash the potatoes, cut into even pieces and boil in salted water until tender (this is when you can insert a knife into the potato but it then falls off if you try lifting it out of the water). Drain the potatoes thoroughly and add the butter, cream, ground nutmeg and black pepper. Then mash thoroughly. Wash and chop the spring onions into small rings using as much of the green as you can. These should resemble giant chives. Mix these into the potato and serve with an extra knob of butter if desired. Alternatively you could turn the potato mixture into a greased earthenware dish, fork over the surface and flash under a hot grill to brown and crisp at the top. But either way, this is the perfect accompaniment to a rich casserole.

Fondant potatoes are roasted in stock, giving a roast potato with the same calories as a boiled potato. Our Managing Director, Peter Stafford, was grazing on these in the kitchen one day. When he asked what they were, I replied "fondant potatoes" - "Delicious!" said Peter. Some weeks later, in a discussion about which potato varieties to plant next season, Peter was enthusiastically planning row after row of... fondant potatoes - we just nodded in agreement...

Candy's Carrot Salad

Named thus, as it is one of Candy Smit's favourite salads. Simplicity itself and fresh, young carrots are the key to the flavour here. No dressing is required.

For 4-6

450g/1lb carrots
110g/4oz sultanas
110g/4oz sunflower seeds
sprig of parsley

Toast the sunflower seeds lightly for 2-3 minutes, but keep an eye on them as they can go from just ready to overdone, just like that. Grate the carrots and mix with the sultanas and sunflower seeds. Add the roughly chopped parsley - a hint of green. Done.

Mixed Bean Salad

Here at Heligan we grow many sorts of legumes - French beans, runner beans, broad beans, peas and mangetouts, as well as beans for drying. In this salad you can use any type of freshly picked beans - raw, blanched or cooked. You could select 3 different varieties of dwarf beans and use them all raw - black, green and yellow beans. This is just a matter of taste.

For 4

340g/12 oz beans
1 small white cabbage
55g/ 2 oz black olives
225g/ 8 oz cherry tomatoes

For the dressing:
4 tablespoons olive oil
1tablespoon white wine vinegar
1 tablespoon clear honey
1 teaspoon Dijon mustard
2 large cloves garlic

Crush the garlic with salt and add to all the dressing ingredients with some black pepper. Shake in a jar until well mixed. Finely shred the white cabbage, chop the beans, mix well together with the olives and cherry tomatoes and add the dressing. Very simple and very tasty.

The black beans go green when you cook them but look great when they are black, so I leave them raw. If they are young, they are very tasty. Should you decide to use them cooked, add to salted, boiling water for about 4 minutes and then plunge into icy cold water, to refresh them. Alternatively, cook them for a few minutes and add the dressing when still hot. Serve as a warm salad, or leave to cool and then serve.

Flora's Green Salad

Named after the great, green lawn in the Northern Gardens, where we don't actually grow any lettuces! The name was only ever just a joke and if it seems a little nonsensical, the recipe is equally so. Throughout the summer many varieties of lettuce, spinach, rocket, endive, sorrel etc. arrive at our kitchen, often in small quantities of several varieties. The obvious thing to do is to make a salad of mixed leaves and the mixture changes from one day to the next, so writing a recipe for this ever-evolving dish seems a little strange! However, the dressing for this and the toasted sunflower seeds do remain constant.

For4-6

1 Little Gem lettuce
1 Continuity lettuce
1 Oak Leaf lettuce
6 sorrel leaves
1 small bunch flat-leaf parsley
1 sprig fennel tops
55g/2oz sunflower seeds

Despite the list of green salad leaves given, feel free to change them according to what is available.

Dressing:

1 tablespoon balsamic vinegar
3 tablespoons olive oil
3 teaspoons clear honey
8 drops soy sauce
pinch of salt
pinch of pepper

Wash and tear the 3 lettuces then place in a colander to drain. Roughly chop the flat-leaf parsley and add this to the lettuce. Add the washed and thinly shredded sorrel leaves and snipped fennel tops. Toss these along with the rest of the leaves and place into your favourite salad bowl. Sprinkle the sunflower seeds onto a baking sheet, place under a medium grill until golden, moving them around with a metal spoon so that they toast evenly. Allow these to cool before sprinkling over your salad.

The dressing is simple - just combine all ingredients in a small mixing bowl, whisk by hand for 2 minutes then pour into a jug. The dressing will in time separate, but this is normal. Just give a brisk stir with a spoon and drizzle over your salad. This dressing will keep refrigerated for at least 6 weeks.

Leek, Goat's Cheese and Puy Lentil Salad

Puy lentils are particularly good in salads, retaining their shape and texture. They also have a beautiful blue-green colour which works as a deep background for a colourful dish. Leeks and goa'ts cheese combine well and the peppers add their extra sweetness as well as a touch of colour. We use St Anthony's, which is a Cornish goat's cheese, but any one will do.

For 4-6

8oz/225g Puy lentils
4oz/110g St Anthony's goat's cheese
4 medium leeks
1 red pepper
1 yellow pepper
150mls/5fl oz olive oil
2 tablespoons white wine vinegar
1 lemon

Firstly rinse the lentils under cold water, place in a pan, cover with ample water, bring to the boil and then simmer gently for about 15-20 minutes, until just cooked. Drain and cool under running water.

Pre-heat the oven to 200°C/400°F/gas 6. Wash the leeks carefully and finely shred. De-seed the peppers and chop finely. Warm the olive oil in the oven and then add the leeks and peppers. Cook for 5 minutes and then remove from the oven and cool. Mix in the white wine vinegar to the oil, leek and pepper mixture. Add to the lentils, season well with salt and black pepper and mix thoroughly. Chop or crumble, the goat's cheese and add to the salad. Finish with the juice of one lemon.

Apple Cucumber Tabbouleh

Apple Cucumber, or Crystal Apple is a small, yellow, round cucumber, which when cut in half looks very similar to an apple. The colour, the crisp flesh, even the seed arrangement is all-familiar. To continue the apple theme we have paired this with apple mint, just one of the many varieties grown at Heligan.

For 4

225g/8oz bulgur (cracked wheat)
85g/3oz red onion
3 apple cucumbers
1 huge bunch apple mint
1 huge bunch parsley
3 cloves garlic
5 tablespoons olive oil
570mls/1 pint boiling water
lemon juice to taste
salt and black pepper

Place the bulgur in a mixing bowl, pour the boiling water over it, give a little stir and set aside for 15-20 minutes, until all the water has been absorbed. At this stage fluff over lightly with a fork, then put in a cool place while you prepare the other ingredients. Peel, de-seed and chop the apple cucumber into small dice. Finely chop the red onion and crush the garlic cloves. Remove the mint leaves from their stalks, wash and chop finely along with the parsley. When the bulgur is quite cool, add the olive oil, apple cucumber, mint, parsley, garlic, onion and salt and pepper. Mix all the ingredients together, then add lemon juice to taste. The important thing with tabbouleh is it should be full of green herbs and have a good lemon flavour.

Richard has quite a passion for apple mint - he once made a delicious apple mint jelly in one of his preserving sessions. These occasions involve stirring a number of 40 pint saucepans until the early hours. Being on your own at Heligan at night is quite an ordeal - he once heard ghostly footsteps at 2am, when armed only with a large spoon. The next morning his ashen face was a sight to see - personally I blamed it on the vinegar fumes!

Chilli and Lime Pilaff

I first made this distinctive rice dish for one of our Feast Nights. I used our own chillies, garlic, onions, herbs and limes. Unfortunately paddy fields were not well documented in Victorian Britain and therefore not part of the Tremayne Estate, so we made do with good quality long grain rice and the result was a great success, with an intoxicating aroma that filled the kitchen. Feel free to experiment with other ingredients, herbs and spices. As long as the rice to liquid ratio is correct, it will always work successfully, and it is so forgiving that once cooked you can turn the oven down and an hour later it's just as good.

For 4

290mls/10fl oz American long grain or basmati rice
570mls/20fl oz hot vegetable stock
1 clove crushed garlic
3 fresh green chillies
55g/2oz chopped onion
2 limes
half a teaspoon ground turmeric
half a teaspoon ground coriander
2 sprigs chopped parsley
2 sprigs leaf coriander
4 bay leaves
28g/1oz butter
salt and pepper

Heat the butter in a paella pan or a large saucepan with a tight fitting lid and a metal handle. Add the onion, garlic, bay leaves, parsley, ground coriander, turmeric and chillies, which have been deseeded and finely chopped (NB: wash hands thoroughly after handling chillies or wear disposable plastic gloves). Cook slowly for 5 minutes. Rinse the uncooked rice in cold water, drain and add to the pan. Cook for a further 2 minutes. Add the juice and zest of 2 limes and a little salt and pepper. Pour in the vegetable stock, giving a brief stir, cover and place in a preheated oven 170°C/325°F/gas 3 for 45-50 minutes, by which time all the liquid should be absorbed. Remove from the oven - add roughly chopped coriander and lightly fluff over with a fork. Serve immediately or hold until required in a low oven covered with a tightly fitting lid.

Other pilaffs I have made at Heligan include mushroom and green olive, toasted nut and date, and lemon and fennel. Just let your imagination run wild.

Wild Mushroom Risotto

A much-enjoyed part of my lifestyle in Cornwall is foraging for wild food. As a chef, I have spent many years balancing food budgets so the idea of "free food" fills me with a warm glow! I had been picking wild mushrooms for a number of years before arriving at Heligan, although I now find myself trying varieties new to me, like clustered grey gills, shaggy ink caps, and two-tone wood tufts. But I have yet to pluck up the courage to nibble on a Jew's ear (apparently named after Judas Iscariot).

For 4

340g/12oz Arborio rice
85g/3oz butter
450g/1lb wild mushrooms (or shop bought exotic mushrooms)
85g/3oz onion
3 cloves of garlic
150mls/5fl oz dry white wine
850mls/30fl oz vegetable stock
30g/1oz pumpkin seeds
1 large sprig chopped parsley
pinch of saffron
salt and pepper

Heat the stock, wine and saffron in a saucepan until just simmering for use later on.

Heat the butter in a large saucepan, cook off the finely diced onion and crushed garlic for 2 minutes. Add the rice and sliced mushrooms and cook for a further 2 minutes whilst stirring. Add one ladle of hot stock, the pumpkin seeds, chopped parsley and season with a little salt and pepper. Cook gently, stirring occasionally and adding more stock as each ladleful is absorbed. Continue this until the rice is thick, creamy and tender (approximately 20-25 minutes). At this stage you may stir some extra butter or even a splash of cream to make this even richer. Taste and season if required. Just wonderful served with ciabatta bread and a few sun-dried tomatoes.

A cautionary note at this stage - only pick mushrooms when you are certain of their identity - it is a good idea to attend some organised mushroom forays and purchase a reputable field guide with photographs. With this said, there are many good mushrooms to try and many a country walk to be enjoyed - happy hunting!

Celeriac and Potato Rösti

Celeriac may look like the ugly sister to the humble turnip, but if you have yet to try it I must encourage you to do so. It is so versatile. Grated, it can be added to salads; diced, it can used in stews and casseroles; it adds flavour and thickness to soups and when puréed with butter and pepper, it is better than swede. Even the stems can be treated like sea kale and the strong flavoured leaves can be used sparingly in salads. Here is one of our favourite celeriac recipes - röstis can be cooked in one piece and cut into portions, as described below, or shaped into individual patties and roasted in the oven.

For 4

340g/12oz peeled celeriac
340g/12oz peeled waxy potatoes
110g/4oz onion
2 tablespoons olive oil
juice of half a lemon
good pinch of salt
freshly ground black pepper
4 sprigs of parsley

Grate the potatoes and celeriac into a bowl, add the lemon juice, season with salt, stir and leave to stand for 10 minutes. Heat the oil in a frying pan and slowly cook the finely sliced onion. Returning to the potato and celeriac mixture, squeeze out all the liquid, add the cooked onion and season with freshly ground black pepper. Re-heat the oil in the pan before adding the rösti mixture, patting out gently to form a flat cake. Fry slowly on a low heat, giving the pan a shake now and then so the rösti does not stick. When the underside is golden brown place a large plate over the top of the pan and tip the rösti over onto the plate. Now carefully slide back into the pan and cook for a further 10 minutes on a low heat. If your rösti is a little on the thick side a further 10-15 minutes in a moderate oven (180°C/350°F/gas 4) may be needed to finish the cooking process. Serve hot, cut into wedges and garnish with sprigs of parsley.

A good well-seasoned or non-stick frying pan is essential for this recipe, and it must have a metal handle.

Oaty Rhubarb and Date Crumble

Rhubarb is not the trendiest of fruit, but when you taste something like this you begin to wonder why we don't eat more of the stuff. We have so much rhubarb here at Heligan in the spring that we are constantly coming up with new ways of cooking with it. I even found an interesting recipe for roast puffin stuffed with rhubarb! I have yet to find a reliable puffin supplier... So we will have to continue with the ever-growing range of desserts and cakes with a rhubarby theme. This is one of the best hot rhubarb puddings, taking the well-known Rhubarb Crumble and giving it a new twist.

For 6

560g/1lb 4oz rhubarb
110g/4oz chopped dates
140g/5oz caster sugar
225g/8oz plain flour
55g/2oz rolled oats
85g/3oz butter
110g/4oz demerara sugar
30g/1oz chopped nuts

Wash and chop the rhubarb into 25mm/1 inch pieces and put these, along with the caster sugar and just a splash of water into a saucepan. Cook until the fruit is softening, but not yet turned to pulp. Then tip into a baking dish and sprinkle the chopped dates over the rhubarb. Place the butter, demerara sugar and flour into a mixing bowl, rubbing in until all lumps of butter are dispersed. Mix in the rolled oats and chopped nuts, using this to cover the rhubarb evenly. (Do not press this down.) Bake in a preheated, moderately hot oven 200°C/400°F/gas 6 for 25-30 minutes until crisp and golden. Serve piping hot with creamy smooth custard or a generous dollop of clotted cream.

Puddings

Strawberry and Apple Mint Yogurt Ice

Fresh strawberries - the taste of early summer - combine with mint to make a refreshing, cleansing and light dessert. You could try this with any fruit; gooseberries, blackcurrants and redcurrants would all work well, although you may want to add some extra sugar or honey if you use less sweet fruits.

For 6-8

570mls/1 pint natural yoghurt
285g/10oz strawberries
30g/1oz vanilla sugar
100mm/4inch sprig of apple mint
2 egg whites

Stir the yoghurt and freeze for about 1 hour. Meanwhile, roughly chop the strawberries and place in a pan with the vanilla sugar and warm for about 5 minutes until softened. Take off the heat, very finely chop the apple mint, add to the strawberries and leave to cool completely. Stir the fruit mix into the semi-frozen yoghurt. Whisk up the egg whites until stiff and then fold into the yoghurt, mix and freeze until completely firm. During this time, remove from the freezer and lightly fold mixture every 15 minutes for the first hour. When it comes to serving, do not forget to let the ice warm for about 15 minutes - it tastes so much better.

Blackcurrant Fool with Cassis

There are some crops at Heligan that are over far too quickly. The soft summer berries are awaited eagerly, enjoyed briefly, then dreamt of longingly for another year. A good way of holding onto those heady days of summer is to freeze a quantity of berries and, although some firmness is lost, there are recipes where this does not matter: for example, mousses and fools. This blackcurrant fool looks very impressive in tall slim wineglasses, and with the addition of crème de cassis, tastes just heavenly.

For4-6

285g/10oz fresh or frozen blackcurrants
85g/3oz caster sugar
290mls/10fl oz cooked and chilled custard
290mls/10fl oz whipping cream
50mls/2fl oz crème de cassis
4-6 sprigs mint

Place the blackcurrants, caster sugar and crème de cassis in a liquidizer for 30 seconds. Whip the cream until it is thick and forms peaks. Place 2 tablespoons of the whipped cream into a piping bag with a star nozzle. Fold the remainder into the cold custard. Pour just a little of the blackcurrant mixture into the bottom of 4 large or 6 small wineglasses. Fold the rest into the cream/custard mix and spoon into the glasses, finishing with a rosette of whipped cream and a sprig of mint. Chill for at least one hour before serving.

Gooseberry Fool

This dessert is so simple I feel a bit patronising telling you how to make it. With pound upon pound of gooseberries arriving in the kitchen during early summer we are constantly striving to find new ideas and exciting recipes, but in this particular case the old one is, without a doubt, the best!

For 6

450g/1lb gooseberries
1 lemon
140g/5 oz caster sugar
275mls/10fl oz double cream
275mls/10fl oz cooked, cold custard
6 mint leaves
6 physalis (Cape gooseberries)

Wash the gooseberries and remove the stalks. Cook them in a pan with the juice of the lemon and the caster sugar. When the fruit is reduced to a soft compote, remove from the heat and leave to cool. Whip the cream until it forms soft peaks and place in a mixing bowl, but keep back enough to pipe 6 rosettes. Fold in the fruit purée and the cold custard (remove any skin that has formed on the custard to avoid lumps in your fool). When smooth and even textured, spoon into tall wineglasses, finishing with a rosette of cream, a mint leaf and a physalis (opened up and hung on the side of the glass). Chill for at least one hour before serving. Best eaten alfresco at the end of a hot summer's day.

Although not available to the garden staff here at Heligan a century ago, we have experimented with growing our own physalis, both outdoors and in the citrus house.

Crème Brûlée with Grilled Peaches

Crème brûlée is a very popular dessert, but as it is so rich it is best served in small portions. I find the addition of fruit cuts through the creaminess and yet complements it at the same time. The peaches grown at Heligan have a very short season but are the height of indulgence so they add a finishing touch to an already classic dessert. I have used vanilla sugar, which we keep in the kitchen all year round. This is caster sugar infused by inserting vanilla pods and leaving for a good few months. A few drops of good quality vanilla essence will do the job just as well.

For 4

2 peaches
440mls/15fl oz double cream
6 egg yolks
2 tablespoons vanilla sugar
4 tablespoons demerara sugar

Crème Brûlée (to be prepared a day in advance)
Warm the cream in a small saucepan until just below boiling point. In a heatproof bowl beat the egg yolks with the vanilla sugar until fluffy and pale in colour, then whisk in the warmed cream. Set this mixing bowl on top of a pan of simmering water. Stir continually until the custard is thick enough to coat the back of a spoon and pour the mixture into ramekins. Put these in a roasting tin with enough hot water to come halfway up the sides of the ramekins. Bake in a preheated oven at 170°C/325°F/gas 3 for 15 minutes. Remove and chill in the fridge overnight. On the day of serving, place on a baking sheet, sprinkle with an even layer of half the demerara sugar and place under a hot grill until evenly browned and the sugar has caramelised, but not so much as to boil the custard underneath. Remove and cool before serving with the peaches.

Peaches: Remove the skin and stones from the two peaches and slice into segments. Place on a baking sheet and sprinkle with the rest of the demerara sugar. Place under a medium grill until sugar has caramelised, then remove and allow to cool.

To serve, place the crème brûlée on a small plate in its ramekin and arrange slices of peach fanning out to one side. A deliciously rich dessert and well worth the time and effort.

Lemon and Basil Cheesecake

You will often hear me sing the praises of fresh basil, but recently I heard a TV chef suggesting that basil went very well with citrus fruits in all manner of desserts. I was eager to try this out and when some lemons started to appear on our own trees in the citrus house, only yards from a patch of fragrant basil... Well, scrumping ensued and a cheesecake was born!

For 6-8

small pack of digestive biscuits
55g/2oz butter
225g/8oz cream cheese
290mls/10fl oz whipping cream
85g/3oz caster sugar
5 lemons
1 small bunch of fresh basil

Grease and line the bottom of a 255mm/10 inch cake tin (the sort with a loose bottom) and crush all but 3 of the biscuits in a bowl, using the end of a rolling pin. Then melt the butter in a pan and mix in the biscuit crumbs. Tip this into the cake tin, spread out and press down firmly with the back of a spoon and chill in the fridge. Put the juice and zest of 4 of the lemons into a bowl and mix in the sugar until dissolved. Stir the cream cheese into the lemon juice until it is of a smooth, even consistency. Whip the cream and fold into the cheese mixture, keeping some of the whipped cream back for piping on the top (enough for 8 rosettes). Finally, shred the basil but keep 8 leaves for garnishing - fold in the shredded basil and spoon mixture onto the biscuit base. Smooth out flat, cover and chill for 2 hours.

While this is going on you can make a nice cup of tea and enjoy the 3 digestive biscuits I mentioned keeping back!

When the cheesecake is quite set, remove from the tin and decorate with rosettes of cream, basil leaves and twists of the last remaining lemon.

Lemon and Lime Parfait

Although we do grow citrus fruits here at Heligan, they are not grown in great abundance, so when we get a trugful of lemons and limes fresh from the tree it's important to produce something memorable. A parfait has the cool refreshing quality of ice cream but the lightness in texture of a mousse. We served small portions of this with an Indian Spiced Fruit Salad. Perfect after hot or spicy food.

For 6

3 lemons
4 limes
3 eggs
290mls/10fl oz double cream
110g/4oz caster sugar
30g/1oz chopped pistachio nuts

Separate the eggs and add the sugar to the yolks. Whisk until they are thick and white in appearance. Stir in the juice and zest of 2 lemons and 3 limes, then whisk the egg whites until they reach soft peaks and add to the egg yolk mix, but don't stir. Whip the cream until thick but not too stiff. Finally fold together the cream, egg whites and yolk mixture with a metal spoon, taking care not too knock out all the air you have whipped into the cream and egg whites. When blended together spoon into a dish or ramekins, sprinkle with pistachio nuts and place in a freezer for at least 3-4 hours.

To serve, remove from the freezer and stand for 4 minutes before garnishing with a twist of lemon and lime. Delicious served on its own or with some fresh exotic fruit like mango, pawpaw or pineapple.

Spiced Fruit Salad

At Heligan some fruits, being more of a horticultural achievement, are rarer than others. When a melon, a pineapple or some passion fruit arrive at the kitchen it is a real occasion and we try to do them justice with imaginative and unusual recipes. This is an Indian version of fruit salad, with delicate aromatic undertones.

For 4

225g/8oz strawberries
3 passion fruits
1 small pineapple
1 small melon
1 kiwi fruit
1 orange
290mls/10fl oz orange juice
2 teaspoons garam masala
1 nutmeg
4 sprigs mint
pinch of salt
freshly ground black pepper

Pour the orange juice into a large glass bowl. Add the garam masala, a pinch of salt and a generous twist of black pepper. Peel and chop all the fruit (except passion fruit), add to the orange juice, stir, and leave to infuse for at least 2 hours. Using a slotted spoon, place a portion of the fruit into the centre of a dinner plate with as little juice as possible. Scoop the inside from the passion fruit and spoon little dollops at regular intervals around the outside of the plate. Repeat for each serving. Finally, grate a little fresh nutmeg over the fruit, garnish with a sprig of mint and serve. Coconut or Indian ice cream goes very well with this.

Eve's Pudding with a Hint of Quince

With many glorious varieties of apples arriving from the garden throughout late summer/early autumn, the hot puddings which use them go down very well as the days grow colder. Served with clotted cream or piping hot custard - desserts like these warm you to the very core and leave you with a healthy glow! We are also lucky to have quinces growing in the gardens. These fruits are quite sharp, but have a pungency that complements the apples wonderfully.

For 6-8

675g/1lb 8oz cooking apples
2 quinces
225g/8oz caster sugar
half a teaspoon mixed spice
85g/3oz butter
2 eggs
170g/6oz self-raising flour

Peel, core and chop the apples and quinces. Place in a large pan with a splash of water and 150g/5oz caster sugar. Cover and cook gently until the apple is just soft but not yet turned to pulp. Remove from the heat, turn into an ovenproof pie dish and spread out evenly. Place the softened butter, the remaining sugar, eggs, half a teaspoon of mixed spice and self-raising flour into a food mixer bowl and beat on a slow speed for 1 minute. Scrape down the sides of the bowl and beat on fast for 2 minutes until smooth and light in colour. Spread the sponge mix over the top of the apple and bake in a preheated oven - 200°C/400°F/gas 6 for 25-30 minutes until the sponge is golden and firm to the touch. Serve hot with smooth creamy custard or, for a real treat, a large dollop of clotted cream.

Oils and Dressings

Marinated oils are a particular passion of mine. This page is not so much a recipe, more a guide to the joys of flavoured oils and the dressings you can create to bring your salads to life. The oils on their own are simple to make with many different culinary uses. For example, brushing juniper oil over salmon or frying ingredients in garlic oil gives wonderful flavour from the start. Use a drizzle of chilli oil on hot pasta. Dressings are another area where your imagination can run wild. My only piece of advice here is to season gradually and taste frequently. You can always add more, but once in, you can't take it away!

Marinated Oils

Start with the best ingredients: olive oil is the obvious choice but feel free to experiment with other oils: nut oils for a Far Eastern blend and grape seed oil and citrus flavours also go well together. To start, wash your bottle in very hot water and then dry in a low oven. Remove and allow to cool before inserting the ingredients of your choice. These themselves must be washed and dried. Top up with your oil of choice and finally seal with a clean stopper or cork. Label and leave for at least 6 weeks before use.

Here are a few examples to inspire you:

juniper and hyssop olive oil
peanut oil with lemon grass and galangal
garlic and thyme olive oil
sunflower oil with rosemary and lemon peel
grape seed oil with cardamoms and cinnamon
walnut oil with sun-dried tomato, oregano and basil

Dressings

Just combine all the ingredients, give a vigorous stir, taste and adjust the seasoning accordingly. These may be chilled for later use.

Tuscan Tomato and Basil Dressing
120mls/4fl oz olive oil
30mls/1fl oz red wine vinegar
30g/1oz finely chopped sun-dried tomatoes
1 small bunch chopped basil
1 sprig chopped oregano
1 sprig chopped parsley
half a teaspoon tomato purée
salt and pepper to taste

Lemon and Roast Capsicum Dressing
90mls/3fl oz olive oil
1 lemon juice and zest
1 sprig chopped lemon balm
1 sprig chopped parsley
half a teaspoon demerara sugar
1 yellow pepper (roasted for 12 minutes, peeled, deseeded and finely chopped)
salt and pepper to taste

Red Pesto

This recipe gives a pungent, light coating not only to pasta but also grilled meats, fish, and roasted vegetables. Basil is the key ingredient in pesto which, when bottled correctly, is an excellent way of preserving this summer herb for use at other times of the year. It also brings a Mediterranean warmth to every dish in which it is used. In addition to this the English physician, Nicholas Culpepper, said in 1862, "Basil being applied to the place bitten by venomous beasts, speedily draws out the poison..." Just the thing for one of my trips down the Jungle picking wild mushrooms.

For 4 or more, depending on how you use it!

2 cloves garlic
1 large bunch fresh basil
55g/2oz walnuts or pine nuts
55g/2oz sun-dried tomatoes
55g/2oz Pecorino cheese (grated)
150mls/5fl oz olive oil
salt and pepper to taste

Place the garlic, basil, nuts and sun-dried tomatoes into a food processor and whizz until smooth. Add the oil slowly with the motor still running. Then add the grated cheese and give a final whizz. Season with salt and pepper to taste and it is then ready to use. Any left over will keep for a week if covered and refrigerated.

Pickled Q

This is not how you will find me on a Friday night (well not that often anyway). It's a simple pickle - very quick and easy and also ready to eat in just 2 days. It will only keep for around 3 weeks, preferably in a refrigerator.

900g/2lb cucumber
570mls/1 pint white wine vinegar
4 bay leaves
1 teaspoon black peppercorns
1 tablespoon black mustard seed
salt

Slice the cucumbers into 5mm/¼ inch slices and place in a colander, liberally sprinkled with salt. Leave to stand for 30 minutes to draw off the moisture, rinse in cold water and dry well. Next place all the remaining ingredients in a non-corrosive pan, bring to the boil and simmer for a few minutes. Place the cucumber slices into hot, sterilized jars and pour the vinegar mixture over, pushing the cucumber down to make sure there are no air pockets. Seal the jar, let it cool, refrigerate and there you have it - pickled Q.

Marrow Chutney

We first made this after our Heligan Harvest a couple of years ago. We were left with a huge surplus of marrows, apples, onions and a selection of chillies. The original recipe had 54lb of marrow so I have condensed it down a little. This chutney is best left for at least three months to mature, so it is just ready for the lean times of late winter and early spring. A perfect and very traditional way of using up the harvest to give you a delicious chutney.

1350g/3lb marrow
1350g/3lb cooking apples
450g/1lb onions
2 cloves garlic
225g/8oz sultanas
110g/4oz dried apricots
55g/2oz root ginger or
2 teaspoons dried ginger
4 tablespoons black mustard seed
2 - 4 fresh chillies
1 tablespoon sea salt
1 tablespoon cinnamon
1 teaspoon ground cloves
1 teaspoon grated nutmeg
850mls/1½ pints cider vinegar
1800g/4lb sugar

Firstly you need to prepare some of the ingredients. The marrow is best peeled if it is large as the skin can be a bit tough, and then diced up. The apples cored and diced, the onions peeled and chopped, the garlic and ginger peeled and crushed and the chillies chopped finely - and deseeded if you do not want too much heat. Roughly chop the dried apricots and sultanas - if you oil the knife when cutting up the dried fruit it won't stick as much. Now just put all the ingredients in a large pan and slowly bring to the boil, stirring fairly often. Reduce the heat to a very gentle simmer and leave for 2-2½ hours, stirring occasionally until the chutney is thick and has a good jam-like consistency. Pour into sterilized jars while still hot and seal with airtight lids. This will make around 3kg/7lb of chutney. It has proved to be a winner.

Beetroot Chutney

Another chutney born out of the Heligan Harvest. During the winter months our visitor numbers go down considerably which allows us a little time to preserve ingredients and hoard for the coming season. This chutney was used with roast beef in our sandwiches and was very popular; equally delicious with a good strong cheese.

1800g/4lb beetroot
900g/2lb cooking apples
450g/1lb onions
zest and juice of 4 lemons
55g/2oz root ginger or
2 teaspoons dried ginger
2 teaspoons sea salt
2 teaspoons black pepper
870mls/1¾ pints distilled malt vinegar
450g/1lb sugar

Begin by boiling the beetroot for approximately 45 minutes until just cooked. Cool and rub off the skins and dice. You can miss this stage but will need to peel and dice the beetroot small and cook the chutney for a little longer. Core and dice the apples, peel and dice the onions and peel and crush the ginger. Put all the ingredients into a large pan, bring to the boil, then reduce the heat and simmer for around 2 hours or until the chutney has a good consistency. Pour whilst hot into your sterilized jars. Delicious and has a beautiful deep colour. Makes around 3kg/7lb of chutney.

Pumpkin and Ginger Jam

This is an old recipe given to me in exchange for one of the squashes grown in the gardens. It is an unusual jam and makes a really good filling for a Victoria sponge.

3150g/7lb pumpkin flesh
870mls/1¾ pints orange juice
7 lemons
225g/8 oz root ginger
3150g/7lb preserving sugar

Peel and dice the pumpkin, removing the fibrous parts and the seeds. You can wash off the seeds and dry roast them with some salt for a tasty snack later. Zest and juice the lemons, saving any pips to put in a muslin bag. Peel and finely chop the root ginger. Place all the ingredients, apart from the sugar, but including the pips in the bag, into a large pan and cook gently for around 30 minutes. Next add the sugar, stirring it until it is dissolved. If you warm the sugar in the oven first it helps to dissolve it quicker and produces less scum. Bring to the boil for a further 30 minutes or until the jam has reached setting point. You can test it by putting it on a cold saucer - if it gets a skin that wrinkles when pushed with your finger, the jam is ready. Leave to cool a little and then, not forgetting to remove the pips in the bag, pour into hot, sterilized jars. Makes around 4.5kg/10lb.

Mincemeat with Quince

This is a far cry from traditional mincemeat, which would have contained minced beef (which must be why mincemeat usually contains shredded suet). This recipe we use for our mince pies at Christmas time. We keep a large container in the fridge and use within 2 weeks of making, rather than jarring it up and keeping for months to mature. Quince has to be one of the most tart fruits and adds a real piquancy to the mincemeat.

1350g/3lb cooking apples
2 large quinces
450g/1lb sultanas
450g/1lb raisins
450g/1lb currants
450g/1lb soft light brown sugar
zest and juice of 3 lemons
290mls/½ pint brandy
1 teaspoon mixed spice
2 teaspoons cinnamon
1 teaspoon nutmeg

Peel, core and dice the apples. Peel and deseed the quinces and chop very finely or grate. Put all the ingredients into a large pan, using only half of the brandy, and bring to the boil slowly. Then simmer very gently for 20 to 30 minutes. Allow to cool, then add the remaining brandy. Adding the brandy at the end retains some of the alcoholic content for that Yuletide cheer.

Partners in Pabulum

Richard Quested
Catering Manager

Paul Drye
Head Chef

Richard Quested grew up in Kent and began life in the catering industry 22 years ago as a kitchen porter, learning the trade from within and having a sideline of being a musician. He has worked in many locally respected restaurants including The Rose and Crown in Stone Street and The Office Wine Bar in Tunbridge (both sadly now changed beyond recognition).

He moved to Cornwall with his wife Mel and two sons Jay and Max and began working at The Lost Gardens of Heligan during Easter 1997. As a devoted vegetarian of 15 years he found at Heligan a great source of inspiration in the productive gardens and has gone on to use this inspiration within these recipes.

Paul says of Richard: 'The lentil guru' is passionate about organic food, obscure pulses and the most burlesque fruit and vegetables.

On entering the catering industry 20 years ago, Paul trained for 5 years at a well respected restaurant (Colleys of Reading, Bristol, Southampton and Lechlade), before moving on to hold the position of Head Chef at a number of excellent restaurants and then Catering Manager for a large corporate catering company.

In 1997, his decision to leave the rat race meant a life-changing move to Cornwall which finally led him to The Lost Gardens of Heligan. He thought he was just starting a new job, but realized he had in fact entered what he calls 'Chef's Heaven'. It now gives him great pleasure to be sharing his favourite vegetarian and fruit recipes here with you.

Richard says of Paul: Culinary adventurer, very skilled and full of enthusiasm for creating real food.

Postcript

Heligan Today

Heligan was first opened to the public just over ten years ago. Our first goal was the restoration of this magnificent Victorian garden. As the garden developed so did our vision of how it would evolve, raising issues that we had not initially considered.

We now occupy two hundred acres, which include the Lost Gardens and surrounding countryside. This land comprises a variety of habitats - mixed woodland, wetlands and hedgerows adjacent to areas of permanent pasture. They offer us a unique opportunity to explore, in some detail, the complicated relationship between countryside management, conservation and food production, with particular emphasis on the balance between the economics and quality of the food we eat.

The management of our productive gardens has demonstrated only too clearly that if you look after the soil you are well on the way to enjoying a quality product. All too often this simple lesson is forgotten in the search for profit.

We are extending this lesson into the management of our different habitats to see if we can find a practicable and sustainable way forward that will ensure a secure future for our countryside, producing food for us to value and enjoy, while preserving habitats and wildlife.

The recipes in this book are a celebration of ingredients that are produced with pride and a commitment to a sustainable environment. This was one of the cornerstones for the start of the organic tradition. I trust you will enjoy the results.

Peter Stafford
Managing Director